SAVAGE FLOWER

Anna B. Sutton

www.blacklawrence.com

Executive Editor: Diane Goettel
Cover Design: Zoe Norvell
Book Design: Amy Freels
Cover Art: "Dagmar" by Kathryn Williams

Published 2021 by Black Lawrence Press.
Printed in the United States.

SAVAGE FLOWER

Contents

for Kate, just because

Postpartum

The barn cat slinks onto the porch and stretches out across a swatch of afternoon sun. Last night, she left a tiny, headless rabbit bleeding on the mat. Did you know a baby rabbit is called a *kit*, short for *kitten*? It's a funny thing, the way we name our progeny. A kitten is not a cat—or a rabbit, even; an infant is not a man. The sun was once something called a *protostar*—an embryo born under the weight of a dust cloud's own collapse. Billions of years later, the barn cat is picking fur from between her toes, and somewhere in the tall grass, a rabbit is missing.

For Shame

I.

Sugar-mint smoke on my lips, that first
Virginia Slims menthol behind the tennis courts
at a football game—thirty yards from a fallow field
where thirty years before, my father charged
an offensive line so many times that the knot
on his brow sunk deep into the memory-meat
of his frontal lobe. *Forget it, father,*
for I have sinned. With cigarette pinned between
prepubescent lips, I blow—don't suck—don't know
yet the power of a hungry inhale, snake swallow
and syrupy release. Smoke spills from the red-hot tip,
dissolves into the thick cinnamon air of October
overtime. But what is smoke and what is just
my own wet breath?

II.

Valentine's Day & this man is asking me if I need
cash—he has it—while he shifts across
the sleet-slick streets of Murfreesboro, TN.

No, I say, *it's fine*. Tonight, my big first time:
we two drunk strangers on a cat-hair-covered futon
slumped on the soggy floor. The bars of its base

flare like ribs against the wall but there's nothing
inside—nothing beating, nothing singing, just
nearby bodies doing their best. Naked,

I can touch the edges of childhood and this man
is thirty, with chest hair & an ex-wife. Here is an empty
Hungry Man platter he's fashioned into an ashtray.

An overturned beer can. A TV on crates. Once more, he
offers to pay me. I tell him, *No*. I promise, *Nothing*.

III.

Bone-white pills & tap water. Anesthesia is optional
if you're old enough. I stare at the clinic's pimpled ceiling

& the Drifters sing *There Goes My Baby*—serendipitous
track list piped through the bulletproof building.

...moving on down the line

Can I erase it all like chalk? The father—soon just a man again.
I told him not to come & this time, he didn't.

wonder where, wonder where, wonder where...

The lie of one night—draining glasses & the way he caught me
when I slipped. His steady hand, sure as a father's. I thought...

Something inside me has shut down like a factory. Lights out for
the last time. Folks gone for good. Only thing left, the scatter

of trapped birds that, out of necessity, built their homes in the rafters.

IV.

At six, I learned of Original Sin, that ink-black stain
                on all our souls. The sexual indiscretion of the first

man & his second wife, Lilith in the shadows. What does it mean

        to be born damned? I can never say it enough—

                Our Father—though I'll finger these beads
                'til their paint rubs off, & at night whisper, Oh God

                        into the darkness of an empty street or the ear

                                of some nameless man.

Mea culpa, mea culpa, mea maxima culpa.

                They told me when unbaptized infants die, they wait

                in Limbo, sit with malformed limbs

                & prayerless mouths. But when He comes for them,

won't He be nothing—a shape
they can't see,

                movement
& light they won't
remember?

City Planning

First, you've got to build a wall—
put all your booze and bending women
just outside and it'll be enough

to keep most people from asking
What's behind those stones?
Tuck your children into corners

or bury them under floorboards or
bind them like feet. Grind up the bones
of your dead so you can build

new bricks. Just be prepared—
the ground you've got to live on
will tighten. You'll see less

of the sky and the air will be sour
with the stench of those stones.
You will run out of things to eat.

Once in a while, a woman might
toss an onion over the wall. Don't
give it to the children. Hide it

under your skirt and eat it
in the middle of the night,
when everyone else is sleeping.

You'll be the only one in town
who knows what onions taste like.

You'll be the only one.

Friday Mass

Ceremonial gymnasium—two hundred children
lined up like empty cups on the yellow-wood bleachers

that opened from the wall—a fist, released. The smoky bite
of incense pouring from the censer never could overcome

the pervasive sweat of adolescence, buzzing fluorescents
drowning out the sound of the penitential act. From my place

at the back—where the unbaptized lot tended
to settle, rooted in Original Sin—the scriptures were

a crow's song. Come spirit, flame tongue, sacrifice
and a list of demands. In class, we were allowed to take

an unblessed wafer, feel it melt against our soft palates—
how I wanted to know the taste when the Word was made flesh.

Playground

The swing set. Beside it,
        Allison arranged us—

Margaret, a mother horse
        on her hands and knees, legs

spread. Emily, a foal. Face buried
        under Margie's plaid skirt.

The rest of us girls waiting
        our turn to be born

before we were broken
        up. Flaking red monkey bars

strung with a few raw
        wood planks, splintered

by sun, stained by lost
        pieces of candy pilfered

from the *caf.* Here, we dissected
        Sister Mary Andrew's sex

talk—how our boys couldn't help
        themselves, found their bodies

in the night. Then ours.
How we must save them

with shut mouths and crossed
legs. Once, I was locked

on the tennis courts with Bradley.
Sister told us we'd stay there

until we learned how to get
along. For an hour,

I sat quiet, watching
Bradley trap and crush

a cockroach with the sweaty
heel of his hand.

Garden of Earthly Delights

Chain link rattle, a line of boys jerk
the dugout fence. Delicate fingers
turn beastly, like talons, mouths

buckling into barbarous
howls. Their parents applaud
from the bleachers. Under care

of a sitter, cover of the occasional clink
of pint-sized bat to ball, my sister and I
slip away with the rest, convent

of bored girls drifting toward
a blemish of undergrowth flourishing
along the creek. We summit to decide

our roles for play. A mother, busy
with mud pies, I barely notice
when a real man enters

our ephemeral home. The other girls
follow some resonant command, return
to bleachers, wiping dirt

from their hands. My sister embarks
on her fatherly duty, a distant thicket,
the promise of a palmful

of berries. The man and I
assess each other. He is tall, pleased
in gray sweats. I am caked

in red dust, kneeling by the creek.
I imagine this is what he saw, though
I am young and memory

is a slippery thing, a crawfish
discovered under a disturbed
rock, then veiled by kicked-up silt.

I was a flash of something
edible. He was a damp hand
holding the stone.

Confession with Toll House and Thunderstorm, 1993

Half-eaten tube of cookie dough
hardening in my desk drawer. I used
to cradle my swollen belly
atop the bright floral bedspread,
listen to the hiss of tires
beyond my open window, the long,
languishing rumble of another swell
of storms moving in. A storm can still
make my mouth water—citric bite
of preserved egg, crystalline crumble
of sugar soaked in roux. At eight,
a bicycle was a gesture of trust
and I broke my promises, cobbled
in the downpour over train tracks—
my parents' imposed boundary—
three dollars and an alibi tucked
in my shirt pocket. I was certain
the clatter of rain would hide
the crinkle of plastic peeled
from the glistening mass, certain
the cool damp could wash me clean.
Knees curled to chest—
a long cramp, a splinter
of lightning. I shaved slivers
with the edge of a stolen spoon,
slipped them onto my tongue

like communion. Forgive me,
chocolate drop, forgive me,
thunder, for forgetting our history,
wiping it clean like a mouth.

For What I Am About to Do

This morning, an angel hangs
by a thread, cartoonish and carved
out of softwood. She twirls

circles above me, manipulated
by the pulse of a ceiling vent. Her purple

dress is airless, static, cut clumsy
as the rest of her. I am laid out below, open-
legged like a pair of discarded scissors

rusting in the grass. My starched hospital gown
smells like driftwood and bleach—natural rot

and our chemical penance. The drugs
are taking effect. If I were an angel, without
the weight of desire, above the realm

of human shame, I would never dress.
My body would be a collection

of little prayers: the mouth of meeting
thighs, hanging breasts like bended knees, folds
of skin that soften the edges of my torso,

thumb print dimples on my lower back—proof
of God's touch. As a young girl, I cradled

a sweater stuffed under my dress. Every childhood
game began or ended with the act of birth. The closet:
a delivery room I exited alone, arms wrapped

around a plastic doll, my fingers stained purple—
grape ice-pop dye. The Valium, the Demerol.

The hum of the medical vacuum like cicadas
in the backyard. Outside my childhood bedroom,
the trees were so tall. They housed a thousand

lives in each of them. Outside this room, there is
an armed guard, bulletproof glass, the rest of my life—

Bear

A canyon of caves looms over the train tracks

like a city block, high rises swollen with lives
you'll never even glimpse. Each bear's breath

echoes from rocky mouths, slumbering five short.

The missing bodies hang from a neighbor's garage,
strung up to let blood. Last summer, a black bear hung

his head through an open window in the downstairs bedroom

and watched my family sleep. As a child, I found a fresh track
in the mud and thought human—saw heavy heel, swell

of arch, five toes—thought barefoot. To break a dancing bear,

trainers would tether her to an iron stage, shoes bandaged
across her back feet, a slow fire heating the floor. To stand

was salvation, survival swaying to the music.

Center Hill

Moon lilt, sloping to shore—tonight
the lake is quiet as a glass of water set

by the bed. Midnight thirst, throat smoked
like straw catching. Matted grass pulsing

like tongues underfoot. Are you here?
Is it quiet? Can I tell you now, there are

bodies sunk in this lake? Let me show you
the chimney ghosting ten feet deep. Before

I came to the water, I was told a man wrapped
in barbed wire was thrown from the bridge.

Even the most beautiful things are full
of our blood. This holler is heavy with sacred

stones and broken glass; its mud was once
a valley—like prayer, waves fall back against earth.

Hurricane Marina

Center Hill Lake

Thousands of silver fish flash like melting ice along the wind-
whipped peaks of the lake in April. I think *pollution*, see *human*

error—but am told otherwise, that each year the lake turns
like a body in bed and the shock is too much for the smaller fish.

At night, the revel of my naked coworkers cannon-balling
from the patio. I swim away, between the foam columns that hold

up the dock, under the lacework of steel. I am never as bold
as in water, never as naked as when dragging my body up the boat ramp

or stumbling drunk down the slick aluminum bridge, my whole world
a clatter of after-hours echoing across the lake. I want to pray, to believe

the stars are just a scatter of light on my inner eyelid, that what is vast
can be held between my fingers—the hills that encircle the lake

are dark and silent as the sky. They only reply in echoes.

Rendition with Two Girls

We were swimming—had jumped off the dock as we tended to do, stripped down after work and plunged, folded hands and faces first, into the greasy water around the boats, water brown with gasoline and fryer oil, suntan lotion, duck shit, remnants of the river's dead—without life jackets or the emptied-out water jugs to sling ourselves over like survivors. If I had called you to come closer, close enough to wrap my legs around, close enough to brace us against the floating dock, my fingers hooked over mossy bars, damp metal vined with snakes, would you have made yourself an anchor? Pulled us down to the lost and found of ancient catfish, where we could lay in the mud and let our dresses slip from our shoulders, let their shadows pass us over, where we could unearth barnacled keys, swap decaying sunglasses and see ourselves in their lenses, moss-stained fingers, bits of grease still buried in our hair? Could we have touched there, without the safety of a wink, without our netted laughter?

The Tender

I slip along the cracked leather
of a 3 a.m. cab like cheap scotch
across a tongue, clumsy

like ice knocked loose
from the bottom of a glass.
The driver asks *Where to?* and

I don't know, deflect, wrist whipping
toward the bartender who's sliding in
next to me. He speaks—I'm sure

they share a wink—after all, it's nearly
dawn and my neckline is low, a thrust
of freckled breasts. The driver asks

Where are you from? and I oblige,
Nashville. My eyelids slick
as moss. He calls me *country*

girl, sings me songs I don't know.
The men laugh before asking
And you, my friend?

The driver answers, *Algeria*;
my tender says, *Morocco*—
there are no more words

between the men. Slow-stepping
across that icy road, I'd had time
to consider—the possibility

of tragedy against the possibility
of sex. Aren't those stones always
weighing themselves in our minds?

I chose to enter an empty bar, to let
a stranger feed me almonds, to leave
with him and drift off

against the ice-scaled window
as two men turned cold. I never have
to dream of war, lines of demarcation

bricked with blood. Violence
doesn't share my bed unless I want it to.

Photographs of Water

A small tidal wave wraps its fingers
around China's edge. There are people watching
from a nearby boardwalk, umbrellas pointed

toward the cloudless sky. In Manitoba, surprise
snow extinguishes corn crops, heavy drifts
resting on dry stalks splintered

by summer's drought. The victim of an avalanche
is laid out, wrapped in shroud, almost ready
to ignite. The Nepali stranger beside him, striking

a match. In Wales, two men search for the body
of a five-year-old girl in the Dovey beds. One floats
face-down in the current, tethered

by the other's grasp. The indiscriminate speed
of the river—that secret-keeper—is rough-hewn
in blue-black, whitecapped.

Nashville

I.
A city of transplants. Wanderers with guitar cases strapped to their backs, blatant as blinking neon signs that line Lower Broad. Robert's boots, the smiling cascade of pigs. Singer-songwriters turn their palms up and we bang ours together. Resigned. Wind-up percussionists. Our roots burrow through limestone, branches long buried by kudzu. Nothing shines for us.

II.
Pilgrims tap their empty glasses against the bar and we oblige.
Always smiling, always tucking the loose hairs back. Pressing the
meat of our palms against our temples in the privacy of the
kitchen. We accommodate each fantasy, whir like a jukebox with
every dropped coin. A thin man sings about leaving and we
wonder what we should have done to keep him. We let that man
strip our rhinestones for something precious, and in return, all of
us were made less brilliant.

III.

Water is the hand of God and mud is your only constant. You offer us up, each of your elements—neon flesh, the guttural thump of our heels against the floor of a honky-tonk, every calloused finger of your fatherless children. You make us an offering because you already know how we'll fade, biodegrade, disappear like fog on the banks once the sun creeps high enough to pierce it.

IV.

What's mine: the playhouse in the backyard, the aluminum slide
that would sear my thighs every summer, the splinters, the rusted
chain of the swing set, piles of concealed cat shit in the sandbox,
wood and aluminum, the bones of something else, waxy
fragrance of magnolia and dirt, ache in my chest when the first
cloud broke, chordal hiss of tires across a dampened street.

V.

On the news, I watch a man cling to a phone pole, bob like a lure, then sink. Water swallows my old street and fills the driveways. My home drinks deep of the cup, then pours itself out. They say to drown is a gift and once you give in, there is peace. Imagine, a body melted to current, carried across the mud, the tangles of kudzu, over this city, into the atmosphere, past any boundaries we ever built.

The Women's Clinic in Antioch, TN

On the outskirts of Nashville, behind
the hospital, a little house. Brick ranch
with a half-moon drive, vertical blinds

just visible behind narrow windows, tinted
and bulletproof. Because there's a picket fence
of protesters; because there's a city full

of god-fearing folks who've taught their children
to hate us; because there are a thousand
tiny white crosses planted on the front lawn

of my grade school. I came here to worship
at the wall of glass and the security guard
behind it, to make my confession, to take

my communion with this congregation
of women—not mothers, not us. *The body
of Christ repels her.* I came to be absolved

by the humming machine—
its cleansing arm extracts a piece of me
that wouldn't even flicker on the screen.

By Accident

I find myself in Tokyo
with the almost father of my almost
firstborn. It is midnight

on a Tuesday in a rose garden
and I am washing my hands—
ladling cool water over the left

then the right, then sipping
from a cupped palm. This would be
a prayer at home, but here it is

forgiveness. The almost father
positions my face by a particular
flower and takes a photo.

Wilmington

If you could forgive the palmetto bugs
blanketing the slick rocks under the dock, the dog
shit left to shrivel on the salt-washed wood, a man

emerging from below, mud-stained to his shoulders,
his cage of crawfish and a look up your skirt, limp
body breaking at the end of the slips, face bloated

and mercifully turned to the reeds, the Riverwalk
could be lovely—if you could keep your eyes
on the current, the clever lilt of little whitecaps

that belied the rush, the dip and tuck of birds
on its surface—in Tennessee, you knew the Cumberland,
Mississippi, muddy hunger widening with every rain,

but the Cape Fear is a filament, a wick, Atlantic finger
digging a road into or out of Carolina.

Tennessee/ Carolina

I.

It's true, I find signs because I look for them, but there are more
carcasses roadside, half-baked by the sun, today, more cops, all
gunmetal gray and flashing blue lights—*stop, slow down*—so I
park under a live oak outside an abandoned gas station, just west
of Florence, South Carolina, and let smoke drip from between my
fingers. A fat, black bumblebee throws itself at my windshield—
my body buzzing. If I keep driving, I'll get to the Motel 6 in
Newport, Tennessee by sunset—time to spare, to wait, to sip
Dickel and calm down.

II.

We spent years, somehow, in the minutes we found: clumsy
hunger on a dirt road, midday desperation when your house was
empty enough. Years, until you were nothing but a fingertip's
bruise on the outside of my right breast, the shadowy indentations
of teeth above my shoulder blades. And I was a single strand of
auburn hair woven into your pillowcase—weft for a brimming
warp—a question that would dangle if your wife ever plucked it
from the sheets, held it between you, saw that it was too light, too
long, not hers.

III.

There's something about blindness on a back road—darkness, but
for the illuminated icons of your dash, the fleeting sweep of
headlights, dew turning to frost, frost weighing weeds into dirt,
something about the crack of footfall echoing from the woods—
feral dogs or deer—something about their hushed witness, our
clouded voices, the tension of our two forms, the air between us
and how its particles quicken as they compress. Something about
attraction and repulsion, the afterglow, that stretch of guilt that
winds around me while I sleep, every time, the ecstasy of a bad
decision, the secret we keep, the curled lip of a lie, how a flameless
coal burns hotter than any fire. Something about contained heat,
something about forgetting.

IV.

I told myself distance, if nothing else, would keep me still. Boxes
scattered across my apartment, and we paired our words: *last
time, no more, fuck you, fuck me.* This morning, two months and
two states between us, I watched the small black letters of your
name thrash against my phone screen, watched my finger slide
across slick glass. I let you tell me how far I was willing to go—
back over the Blue Ridge, almost the entire way home.

V.

My cigarette spent. The black bee gone for soft pollen. I stare at the pile of hastily-gathered supplies—half-empty bottle of whiskey, two shiny plastic heels piercing the side of a grocery sack, a bottle of cheap perfume—the miscellany of our missed connection. I am not going to Newport. I am not going back to Tennessee.

Rabbit Pen

A foxhole: chain link fence posted around the back
of the guest house, at the far end of our yard—
cement poured a foot deep, chicken wire and a tarp
stretched across the top—we built those rabbits
a fortress, but they always found their ways out.
Or something got in. Two females and a male and
a new litter of kits every week or so. Daily visits
from the neighbor's dog, a stray cat. A hawk diving
nearby was a heart attack. Hundreds of rabbits
were born and died on my childhood lawn, a lesson
in never loving the living. Not without a fence,
the sharpened distance between me and what bleeds.

Mattress Stitch

I forgot not just names but all the faces
and pimpled backs, the variety

of futons and that same smoky damp
that hangs in every college apartment like the last grunt hangs

in the slick air of an eggshell bedroom.
I kept stitching—one lip to the other,

each finger to its opposite, the knots of knees
and inner ankles—together. I made partners

for every piece of me. But basted thread
is long and loose, a placeholder for more

careful work. Sutures pop and oxygen
turns me red raw. If I had known instead

to burrow like a clam
or blacken my windows with ash...

Origami-Inspired, Self-Assembling Robot Crawls by Itself

Time-lapse blossom, swell
and fold—rise up and render
yourself useful. Clumsy crab

shuffle across the table
of your making, foolish
fixture to think that simply

pulling your panels together
could be enough—a dance,
a pittance. A street corner

and an upturned cap. *Come see
the magic metal lily, watch it
crest and fall!* Every movement

like breathing—miraculous, forgettable.

Two Whooping Cranes Are Found Shot Dead in Hopkins County

I've never been close enough to a man
and a gun to see the way a shell disappears

from its chamber, but I can imagine the hot knife
of sound; the two lithe bodies plummeting

into a lake; the dog, her teeth curled
around the neck of the first crane—hunger

has been trained out of her. This is what
I imagine, though the authorities call it

a *thrill kill*, summon the image of a different
mouth, a perfect black O steadied against

the bed of an old truck, limp gray bodies
left behind. When the reward is offered,

authorities are sure to mention that the pair
had mated for life, that the male was found

picked apart by scavengers, a few feet
from its female—found alive, kept alive

for a handful of days. Her body littered
with shrapnel. A thousand miles east,

another clutch of eggs is hatching, another
apology, another bloodless puppet teaching

the little cranes to eat, to fly, to leave.

Gemini

Two-headed dolphin pup washed up
on the shore—pink heads split like legs
opening. Two dead mouths smiling

where I expected feet. A single fin
stiff with weeds. Conjoined couplet—color
of nail beds, early melon—be sure, there are

as many horrors in the ocean as there are
on land. I can't stand to think of you alive
for even a moment after spilling out

into saltwater, struggling to swim while
your mother made the grim decision to leave.
I hope you were gone long before then, hope

holding each other close in the womb—
inverse of the ocean: warm, shallow, and sugar-sweet—
a chorus of blood and breath sung you to sleep.

Hometown

What we called love, I call a dead jellyfish crusted
in gray-gold Atlantic sand—something children toss

at each other once the birds have carried off the poison,
long ribbons dripping with salt and venom. What was touch

is the length of the Blue Ridge Mountains' tubercular spine.
How a park bench in November was your hand, each unrelenting

plank refusing to give. How my body looked elsewhere
for softness—to the black dirt, the ryegrass, finally,

the ocean. Middle Tennessee reached for coastal Carolina
in the bed of my truck. The tidal hush of feet in an empty house—

I never understood ownership until I left you. Then, everything
was mine. The old mattress tucked into a back room—mine. Mine,

the small collection of flatware. The rotting deck, the salt
in my nostrils—mine, mine. When I walked the shoreline searching

for the jagged cut of a dorsal fin, I found one—a six-foot shark
circling the breakers. And then, she too was mine.

Inheritance

Your mother's body leaves first—
withers beneath an outer layer that thins

and yellows. The pockets of fat
her children buried their damp

faces into melt like ice. Even her bones
powder under the weight of themselves.

The body—like anything else—
is a lie, a tool, a crude measurement

of survival. It sheds what is useless
and in the end, everything is. Even you,

with your pert breasts and fresh
blood, will mean nothing soon enough.

Hold tight your own arms, keep yourself
together with plastic and glue. Tie your plump

flesh like a roast. She's been trying to tell you—
the body won't come back once it's gone.

God, He Made You This Way

My father prays for children who aren't
so smart and emails to let us know

we are: *too smart for Jesus*—God!
Too smart for love.

Ever since the seizure, the cloudy
x-ray clipped to the light box, ever since

the surgery (not as successful
as we had hoped), and chemo

he wants:
      a wedding
      a grandchild
      a second drink—three fingers of bourbon on ice

Instead:
      his mother calls
      from her hospital bed
      thinks she's in Augusta
      that her dog has run away

And I want to tell him
      his brain's a thoughtful organ
      to eat itself before time can.

But,

I have his shoulders—round and tilted
toward the wind—his golf ball cheekbones,

furrowed brow. *What else?* I swear, I feel
my own hard tumor growing

slow against my temple. Today, I thought
I was going blind. Tomorrow, I might

pray. But if I say *Thank God,*
I mean *Don't let us die.*

If I say *I love,* I mean *Save me.*

Side Effects

after Yaz®

Like a knock on the door.

The crispy snap
of aluminum as each
pale pill pops

from its case. One
every morning, every day,
for as long as you both shall live

in sin. A billion tiny blood cells
to blame it on, a billion
reasons why. Leah's head

against the bathroom floor
like a thunderclap. I'll bet
she saw lightning. A constellation

of scars across my torso.
They said it wouldn't leave
a mark. They used lasers, little

hooks to grab at my gall
bladder, to drag it out. That's all
they'll take, if you're lucky.

The operating room is an altar
and they are counting up
our organs, embolisms, deep

vein thromboses and hearts
that shuddered before they
stopped. In their defense,

I am just a percentage.
She was a fraction.

Pseudocyesis

To carry grief in the belly

for nine months—breasts swollen

with milk. To hear a heartbeat

where there is none but

your own, feel a blinking presence

in the salt lake of your abdomen.

It won't be a mystery

to the doctor who slices

a smile across your lap, tells you

about a dog nursing a row

of stones. Nature plants its ghosts

inside us sometimes.

Ten Ways That Elephants Are Like Us

1. I wrap damp fingers around the hem
of my mother's dress. They unknit
and she is lost to me—I stumble
through the crowd, reaching out.

2. A bull rarely stays with a herd—
no longer a juvenile, he is shuttled off
in search of mates, wanders between
families, his bloodline a river.

3. When my grandfather died, his wife bent
over the casket, rested her head on his chest,
kissed him. She wanted to hold his hand, but
his fingers would not come undone.

4. A bone removed and carried, the elephants
will often lay grass, leafed branches across
their dead. They inter, remember—a mother
that has lost a child moves slowly for weeks.

5. He says *don't cry*, says *if you cry,
I will cry*. He lays his body close,
breath across my turned cheek. He wants
to understand darkness, reaches for constant.

6. A flash of color and they might remember
a spear lobbed into their midst. They hold
anger in their gut like a child—let it expand,
grow lungs, and finally, tear its way out.

7. Weeping used to be an expression of grief.
Now, it partners with any swell—a mother
embracing her child in a movie, a guttural laugh,
and yes, a loss—I slip into that river like a sound.

8. Language is not lost on the elephants—
they hear danger in the way a tongue snaps
against a fence of teeth. In the distance, a finger
points toward the herd and they know then to run.

9. I try to sign my name with the pen clenched
in the wrong fist, imagine left-handedness—
a world ruled by my opposite. Left-handed, I am
small and quiet. There, I can laugh without crying.

10. Her face is marked and she is shown
a mirror. She lifts her trunk and runs its end
across the mark—recognizes what is wrong
with her image, tries to wipe away the inky scar.

What I Know of Love

I.

My psychologist asks me *You know
that feeling when your heart skips*

a beat? Apparently, it isn't love,
just childhood trauma—like echoes—

bouncing around our insides. It feels right
because it's familiar, like jeans

that haven't been washed in weeks
and smell of rainwater around the ankles.

II.

My parents would lock the door to their bedroom
every few months, during a rainy Sunday or after

a party. Barricaded from their passing romance,
I wondered if bodies fit together like wooden joints.

III.

Amazing how your thumbs
dwarf mine, how the constellations
of looping hairs on your chest—
damp with sweat—can feel so soft
against my shoulders. And how,
in the mirror, we look like people in love:
your arms wrapped around my waist, my arms
wrapped around your arms. We could choose
to stay this way. We don't have to ask why
we're looking in the mirror in the first place.

IV.

You should know, there is something called *dark matter*—missing mass—that accounts for everything

we can feel, but not measure. And *dark energy,* whose scalar fields are divorcing our atoms

at accelerating rates. Relief comes at the end, when we are spread so thin that we won't need

to struggle for such unreasonable reconciliation.

V.

An attachment, or
affection, or concern
born of kinship
or sexual desire.

Or a deeply seated need
to find what we haven't,
the stubborn insistence
that we can.

VI.

Your body, always
a few degrees above average.
At night, our bed is damp and small.
I feel inside the sticky summer
of my childhood—that inescapable
heat, my submission to it.

Boy Returns to Water to Wash Sand from His Feet

Flame. Vein. Fissure.
The lightning strikes a nearby

pier and electrifies
the shore, shocks his body
to still—and you wonder

why I'm so afraid
of living. When the sky
opens up to remind us that, no,

the vast Atlantic is not
impenetrable; it isn't just what cuts
circles in the water around you

that you should fear.
When three commercial jets
come down in a summer.

You tell me it's safer
than barreling down a highway,
but the sky wants you to know

it is not your heaven. It will
rain on you however it can
until you begin to understand.

It will tell the ocean
to rise toward the clouds
and swallow your beach house.

It has sacrificed your son.
You should have painted
blood on the jamb.

I opened my artery
and sugar poured out—lucky,
I'm childless. Lucky,

cyst-riddled. Lucky to know
so well what's got my number.
In the mountains,

the trees bend like spinsters,
boughs branching their fingers
to the dirt. Lucky, what struck here

was sickness, slow and grounded in stone.

Picking Up the Dog from the Spay and Neuter Clinic

We argue. You tell me
she'll be fine in the bed
of the truck; I want her
in the cab with us. I start
to cry; I win
the argument. You tell me
I can't keep trying
to control everything
and I laugh against
the passenger window because
there is so little that I have
a handle on. The dog pisses the seat.
At home, I turn her over, examine her
shaved belly. I had expected
the wound to be bigger.
Three whole organs slipped
through a two-inch incision—
the end of the line.
I had expected
love to be more clearly defined—
a contour drawing in black
permanent marker. What is
the outer edge? The farthest
from each other any two points
can be and still be a part
of one single thing?

What is the clearest way to tell you
that my love is an oversized shoe—
a poor fit? A pain?
How many times do I need to explain
the difference between *depressed*
and *depression* before you understand
why I'm so afraid of leaving
our someday children
in a parking lot?
Why I envy the dog? Listen.
When I was young, my father had to bury
four of our dalmatian's weakest puppies
under my tree fort. Someone else's children
are playing house on the bones.

A Haunting

The dog, always trembling, built herself
a den of discarded laundry under our bed—
she bit you once—that's how I knew our house

was full of ghosts. While you were away
at work, she'd stand at the top of the stairs
and whimper or pace the peeled linoleum

by the basement door until I reemerged.
At night, we'd hear her fighting something furious
in the living room. Hours later, a bodyless

knock on our door. Her terror was gnashing—
wet froth, brindled fur stiff as quills. She didn't sleep
and neither did I. When we moved, I wondered

what shadows would stitch themselves
to our feet, what creeping dark we'd carry
with us like a box of books, like a bruise.

House People

A weekend spent sleeping in, repotting
herbs in the backyard in a late-summer

storm—constant, gentle. We try to teach
the dog not to be afraid of the wet grass

that needs cutting, not to chase the outdoor
cat, who languishes on a patio chair

when he's not slipping through
the neighborhood, drinking from puddles.

The only one of us unencumbered
by bricks, he lopes home like

a drunk, scratched up from a fight.
He disembowels a nest of birds and

brings one to my feet. His indifference
is bloody and insinuating—no matter

how tightly we've woven the twigs,
we are not safe here.

Egg

Twin yolk trembling in the glass crater
of my little mixing bowl, good luck

to some. Two marigold orbs, delicate
as grief—to most, it is the happy herald

of pregnancy; elsewhere, a double ovum
can be an omen of death. Looking down

at the pair—one couched in the other's
soft flesh, membrane spread and narrowing—

I consider leaving them, setting the bowl
in the cupboard until the twins sallow

and dry. Instead, I carry it to him, trimming
the overgrowth along our fence. He shrugs

and tells me it's no miracle—a young chicken
learning to lay or an old girl in a hurry. Deflated,

I return to the kitchen and pierce the tender skin
of the top yolk, watch it weep into its other.

I've Never Loved You More

I'm searching this house
for metaphors—yellow milk, *jus*

that's turned to gelatin
in the far corners

of the refrigerator. When exactly
did we move from one room

to another? There was a time
when my legs were shaved and

clutched at tense angles, like a fist.
I used to be good at that:

close and open.
I don't know why

I'm always shutting my door. *Our* door.
Our house. *Our* dog, with her sad-sack lids

and night terrors. With her, we practice
the transfer of love to sweet

and stupid repercussions. The aftermath
of an afterglow. A street lamp's corona

that fades against the sunrise, only
a little machine to get you through the night.

Ode to a Dead Bouquet

This morning, into the waste bin with you—
two dozen small pink roses desiccated by draft

creeping through cracks in the old hopper window.
Last week, delivered already on your last legs. I'm sorry

I couldn't keep you somewhere warm. It's winter, you know—
you arrived only a day after the frozen rain stopped,

while glass panes still crackled with thaw. Procreated
product of four days of weathered isolation, until I stood

in the doorway of our bedroom and asked him to show me
love. Little things, little pink blossoms piped with violet—

on Monday, you arrived; on Wednesday, he painted
our names on the kitchen wall. Flower as seed, as first

step, as omen, as admiration. A thing of beauty that
blossoms even as it withers. Though each day

you've wilted, darkening heads bowed more
toward my desk, aged and musky with rot,

I want to sew you into my hair, bury you
in my womb, fill my shoes with your powdered petals.

Instead, I've dropped you into the crowded bin,
rinsed your vase and wiped it dry. I'll carry it home

and set it on the counter. An open mouth.

Fertility with Multiple Diagnoses

We are trying to conceive so I stop
taking my antidepressants reduce
that miniscule risk while my doctors
tell me it would be easier if I lost
weight but also that the glitch
in my system will make that loss
near impossible without edging up against
an eating disorder that my hormones
are just as out of whack
as my brain chemistry I was a late
bloomer but when I bloomed
it was a savage flower I bled
for sixteen days that first time
then a few months later through
an overnight pad and heavy denim pant
in under an hour bright detritus dripping
down the plastic legs of our family
computer chair I had been lost
in careful calculus sexual awakening
via A/S/L when my sister came to tell me
my time was up and I'd stained the carpet
when asked how much a woman
should bleed an expert will hold up
a measuring cup and point
to the lowest line when asked how often
a thirty-three-year-old major depressive
will obsess over her looming death

while also trying to flint damp kindling
to fire they will refer you to a specialist
a year ago under fluoxetine's tender watch
I told my mother that if we conceived
I'd be happy and if we couldn't
I'd be fine but then I gave the rest
of my scrip to our dog whose slavering
anxiety is so similar to mine my husband
blames it on *her mother* the very same man
who took a long look at my ovulation
test and said *this seems*
positive what are we doing trying
to make something that might
kill me or more likely husk from me
just as I've gotten my hopes up
what is the cause of all this wrong-set
stuff what should I do when my doctor says don't
think about it too much but also
make sure you're tracking your cycle
when lately I don't know one woman
who's had a child the old-fashioned way
head down and slipped from her
while her doctors tell her *keep going*
you're doing it one more push

Ode to a Wreck

Praise to my ovaries, those broken
little bee hives busy with trying. I'm sorry

I've been so cruel to you, calling you
curse. I should have laid out the red

stains in my underwear like unearthed
texts, treasured their hidden messages, pressed

warm hands to my abdomen to say
thank you, thank you. Twenty years

we've been working on something awful
and I never once commended your efforts.

No wonder you're tired. No wonder
I have to shake you from slumber

every month with a dose of doctor's orders.
Can you forgive me? Like a late-in-life

husband, I'm trying to be better, to compliment
your soft pink surfaces, pocked with cysts,

to feed you and stroll with you past
a winter park just beginning to bud.

Good Health

Bear Creek, NC

The muscles in my lower back
have trained themselves to spasm

around a large cluster of nerves, bundled
like a horse's tail at the base of my spine.

There are cysts—small sacks of fluid
that fill and deflate at random—scattered

across my body: on my ankle, my wrist,
my neck, inside my breasts, dotting the outside

of my ovaries like continents seen from space.
My legs are heavy with the husks of dead veins.

A blood vessel has burst on the bottom of my foot.
Every so often, my brain tells my heart that it's dying,

and my heart believes—follicles rise along my arms,
my lungs stutter, my stomach turns cold. But still,

here we are standing at the end of a rotting dock,
the dog's leash slack in my right hand, your fingers

laced into my left. Here, we are breathing in
the thick marsh, the only light blinking distant

from nearby windows. We'll sleep there tonight—
all I'll know of my body, its proximity to yours.

Conservation

The hand is a bird, or
is painted like a bird. See, inside

the white jumpsuit is a man pretending
to be a woman pretending

to be a bird. The young brown cranes
are learning to eat. The man dips

his hand into the tall grass and pecks
at the mud. *See?* he whistles.

They are learning how to whoop.
They tilt their heads back and suddenly

their bodies are reeds in the wind, whistling.
Brown downy, do they know

how in that instant, they might be
the last of their kind? How alive

we can remain when we don't know
what little space we occupy in time?

Acknowledgments

Thank you to the Traveler's Club—my beloved coven—without whom I could not write or, frankly, exist. To Jacob, who is the inspiration for any hopeful words in this collection, and to all the other family and friends I love, who have loved me back, for keeping me above water.

To the many amazing poets who have helped me shape these poems and this long-simmering manuscript—Eric Tran, Gabriella R. Tallmadge, Regina DiPerna, Jade Benoit, Jamie Mortara, Sally J. Johnson, Sarah Messer, Lavonne Adams, Mark Cox, and many others. Thanks to my blurbers for their generosity—Emilia Phillips, Emma Bolden, and Blas Falconer. To UNC Wilmington, the Vermont Studio Center, Sewanee Writers Workshop, and Tin House Writers Workshop for giving me time to write.

Thank you especially to Black Lawrence Press for believing in this book and finally giving it a body.

Poems in this collection first appeared in the following publications, which I thank for their early support.

Postpartum, *Superstition Review*, Issue 13
For Shame, *Pinch Journal*, Fall 2014
City Planning, *Yemassee*, Issue 18.1&2
Friday Mass, *The Boiler*, Summer 2015
Garden of Earthly Delights, *failbetter.com*, April 2020
For What I Am About to Do, *Third Coast*, Issue 38/39

Bear, *Waccamaw Journal*, Issue 14

Center Hill, *The Boiler*, Summer 2015

Hurricane Marina, *Columbia Journal*, January 2020

Rendition with Two Girls, *Word Riot*, July 2015

Photographs of Water, *Barrow Street*, Winter 2013-2014

By Accident, *Atticus Review*, June 2020

Wilmington, *failbetter.com*, April 2020

Tennessee/Carolina, *Brevity*, Winter 2015

Mattress Stitch, *Stone Highway Review*, Issue 3.3

Two Whooping Cranes Are Found Shot Dead in Hopkins County,
The Southeast Review, Volume 33.1

Gemini, *Copper Nickel*, Issue 21

The Women's Clinic in Antioch, TN, *Quarterly West*, Issue 82

Hometown, *Indiana Review*, Summer 2016

Inheritance, *Cactus Heart Journal*, Issue 8

God, He Made You This Way, *Tinderbox Poetry Journal*, Volume 1,
Issue 3

Pseudocyesis, *Animal Literary Magazine*, March 2020

What I Know of Love, *Wyvern Lit*, Haunted: Volume Two

Boy Returns to Water to Wash Sand from His Feet, *Rust + Moth*,
Spring 2015

Picking Up the Dog from the Spay and Neuter Clinic, *Sundog Lit*,
Issue 5

Egg, *Word Riot*, July 2015

Ode to a Dead Bouquet, *Columbia Journal*, January 2020

Fertility with Multiple Diagnoses, *Booth*, June 2019

Ode to a Wreck, *Columbia Journal*, January 2020

Good Health, *Tupelo Quarterly*, Issue 8

Conservation, *Pinch Journal*, Fall 2014

Photo: Jasper & Fern

Anna B. Sutton was born and raised in Nashville, TN. She received her BFA from the Appalachian Center for Craft at TN Tech and her MFA from UNC Wilmington. She was awarded a James Merrill Fellowship from Vermont Studio Center. Her work has appeared in *Indiana Review, Copper Nickel, Los Angeles Review, Quarterly West, The Offing,* and other journals. Her debut collection, *Savage Flower,* won the St. Lawrence Book Award from Black Lawrence Press. Anna has worked for literary organizations including Blair Publisher, Humanities Tennessee, Lookout Books, One Pause Poetry, Writers in Action, Young Writers Workshop at UNCW, and the Tennessee Young Writers Workshop. She also co-founded The Porch Writers Collective in Nashville and volunteered as an editor or reader for numerous literary magazines, including *Dialogist, Ecotone,* and *Gigantic Sequins.* She currently lives with her growing family in Winston-Salem, NC.